This book belongs to:
Brayden

Hello, my name is Neymar da Silva Santos Júnior!
Whew, that's a mouthful!
Just call me Neymar.
I'm one of the biggest athletes in the world,
leading my soccer team to win.

I love soccer since I was a little kid.

Amazon River

Brasilia

Pantanal

Sao Paulo

Cataratas
do Iguara

BRAZIL

I was born in Sao Paulo.
For those who don't know,
that is a state in the country
of Brazil.
We have 26 states in all.

My father, who is also called Neymar,
was a soccer player and he saw that I had
his love for soccer too!

He encouraged me to play soccer.
He gave me advice like he was my coach.
Ever since I was little, he helped me improve my skills.

My father never stopped encouraging me,
and he turned me into the all-star I am today.

I played all kinds of soccer!
First, I loved to play futsal.
Futsal is indoor soccer.

I also loved street soccer. I'd play outdoors with friends, and I'd always impress my pals whenever it was my turn to score.

When I was 11, I joined a Santos FC,
a soccer club, and took off as a young star.

Soccer is a big business in Brazil.
Even so, I didn't play soccer for the money.
I did it because I loved the sport.

The thrill of chasing the ball, the energy
you feel when you score the goal,...
was why I loved playing soccer so much.

When I was 17, I signed my first pro contract.

In my first season, lost my first game,
and I felt a little sad because of that.
But I knew not to give up!

I kept playing, and soon, I led my team to victory across many seasons.

I realized to win, you must always practice.
Talent doesn't come to those who sit around.

Every day, I would practice.
I practiced with friends, by myself, at home,
or outside.
Any chance I could get to improve, I took it.

I had a dad who wanted to help me,
and I listened.
Odds are, you have someone in your life
who wants you to succeed, too.
Listen to them, and you may become
as big as me one day!

Find someone who will help grow your skills.
Do you want to be a painter?
Find a talented artist and ask for help.
Do you want to fix cars?
Talk to a mechanic.
Do you want to be a soccer player?
Watch and learn from me!

Just keep practicing, and you can
be anything you want.

Did you read about my friends, Ronaldo and Messi, yet?

CPSIA information can be obtained
at www.ICGtesting.com
Printed in the USA
LVHW070317291018
595060LV00004B/71/P